Denver and The Doolittle Raid

The Extraordinary Story of an Ordinary World War II Hero

Denver and The Doolittle Raid

The Extraordinary Story of an Ordinary World War II Hero

Bo Burnette

Denver and the Doolittle Raid

Copyright © 2012 Bowen D. Burnette

Published by Tabbystone Press

Tabbystone Press

All rights reserved. No part of this book may be reproduced or transmitted in any way—electronic or mechanical—without the written permission of the publisher, except where permitted by law.

Cover image is *Into the Arms of the Dragon* © William S. Phillips. Courtesy of the artist and the Greenwich Workshop, Inc.

ISBN: 978-1-7325924-3-8

Third Edition

Printed and bound in the United States

Also available in eBook editions

*Dedicated to the memory of
Denver Vernon Truelove
1919-1943*

Acknowledgements

Much time, travel, and research went into writing this book. Denver's sister, Blanche Truelove Bowen, who is my great-grandmother, was a wonderful help in editing, getting pictures, and providing first-hand information about Denver's life. My mom and dad encouraged and helped me as well; my mom especially helped with editing. I owe a special thanks to them. My oldest sisters, Kendall and Courtney, helped with editing, and the book wouldn't be the same without their input. They, along with my other sisters, Kelley and Susanna, encouraged me and picked up my slack while I researched and wrote.

Many thanks to David Schlender, who created an amazing cover for this book. I am also grateful to Josiah Dooley, who drew a fantastic logo for my publishing company, Tabbystone Press.

I have much appreciation for William Phillips and the Greenwich Workshop for allowing me to use Bill's remarkable painting, *Into the Arms of the Dragon*, on the book cover.

I am also appreciative of Todd Joyce, son of Doolittle Raider Richard O. Joyce, for all the information I gathered from attending the reunion in Omaha, Nebraska, coordinated by him in 2011. He has a great website about the Doolittle Raid: www.doolittleraider.com.

Special thanks go to Mrs. Cindy Chal, and her father, Raider Lt. Col. Richard E. Cole, who helped me with information, editing, and pictures for this book (including the second picture of the *Hornet* in chapter three). In addition to Dick Cole, I would like to thank all the Doolittle Raiders and their families, especially those still with us at the time of writing: David Thatcher, Tom Griffin, Ed Saylor, and Bob Hite.

I owe a huge thanks to Russ Jacobs, who kindly served as my historical advisor and editor in the final stages of the book's publication. Without him, the book would not be what it is today.

Finally, I am especially grateful to Doolittle Raid historian, Col. Carroll V. Glines, for proofreading my book and giving me invaluable suggestions. Since Col. Glines has written multiple books about the raid and is an honorary Raider himself, I feel that he is the definitive authority on the raid.

Most of all, I want to thank God for His work throughout this project and in my life. He supplied everything that made this book possible.

Preface

There are a large number of children's books about famous Americans such as George Washington, Daniel Boone, and many others. Almost every kid has heard the stories of these heroes. But what about the lesser known people, who also have incredible stories? Who will put their stories into print?

My great-great-uncle, Denver Vernon Truelove, is one of these lesser-known American heroes. He was simply a farm boy from Georgia, but he daringly served his country in the Doolittle Raid during World War II. Of the many children's books that run off the presses these days, more should give tribute to normal yet extraordinary Americans who gave their hearts and even their lives for their country. My purpose is to make him and those he served with known, and to encourage others to promote the stories of these great patriots.

Bo Burnette
April 2012

Contents

1—Attack on Pearl Harbor _____ 13

2—From Schoolboy to Soldier _____ 19

3—Aboard the *Hornet* _____ 29

4—Off to Japan! _____ 35

5—Farther Into China _____ 45

6—Home at Last _____ 51

7—Denver's Final Mission _____ 57

8—A Continuing Legacy _____ 65

Author's Notes _____ 73

Appendix: Doolittle Raid Crews _____ 77

Bibliography _____ 93

Index _____ 99

1
Attack on Pearl Harbor

It was the year 1941. The Allied nations of Great Britain, France, the Soviet Union, and China were engaged in war against the Axis powers of Italy, Germany, and Japan. While the United States was manufacturing planes and other military supplies for the Allies, it had not yet entered the war, remaining neutral. Many Americans wished to keep the country out of the war, since it had experienced World War I, then known as "the Great War," just a few decades earlier. However, circumstances would soon occur that would propel the country into World War II.

On December 7, 1941, just before the Japanese officially declared war on the United States, Japanese bomber planes attacked Pearl Harbor, Hawaii. Originally, their intent was to declare war and *then* attack. However, the message could not be transmitted to the United States government in time, so the attack seemed all the more horrendous to the unsuspecting Americans. It resulted in the bombardment of hundreds of ships and aircraft and the merciless killing of many American soldiers and sailors.

14 | Denver and the Doolittle Raid

The Japanese Attack on Pearl Harbor in Oahu, Hawaii (USN Photo)

As hundreds of Japanese planes swooped down upon the Hawaiian island of Oahu, thousands of servicemen were forced to run for cover and abandon ship. Even so, many did not escape with their lives, and countless more were wounded. This attack was an incredible blow, especially to the United States Navy, because Pearl Harbor was an important naval base. War now seemed inevitable.

This sudden, violent Japanese assault infuriated Americans, especially President Franklin D. Roosevelt. Congress declared war on Japan the next day. The United States was now officially in World

War II as a part of the Allied forces. President Roosevelt announced by radio the declaration of war to the listening nation.

President Franklin Delano Roosevelt signing the declaration of war on Japan (U.S. Government Photo)

Pearl Harbor was a devastating attack and a significant strike to the morale of the American people. However, there was some hope. Providentially for the United States, all three of the Pacific

Fleet aircraft carriers were out to sea at the time of the attack. These ships would soon be instrumental in carrying out a secret retaliatory raid that America was planning and would change the face of the United States Navy forever from a battleship navy to an aircraft carrier navy.

After the Pearl Harbor raid, President Roosevelt called his top military staff together and announced his desire for a secret aerial raid on the Japanese home islands. The Japanese had to be stopped from augmenting their empire, so the Americans began to formulate a strategy.

Navy Captain Francis S. Low had seen Army bombers taking off on a runway that had a carrier outline painted on it. As Low watched the planes practicing on this "carrier," an idea began to form in his head for Roosevelt's desired raid. He immediately notified those in charge of planning the project.

What was the plan for retaliation? It was determined that the best method of attack was to launch B-25 Mitchell bomber planes, selected for their size and reliability, from an aircraft carrier to drop bombs on Japanese cities. Army aircraft had never before taken off from a naval carrier, so this would be a big—and daring—first try at a new tactic. If successful, it would be a great boost to American morale and might allow the United States to gain the upper hand in the Pacific.

Lietenant Colonel James Harold Doolittle, who became the leader of the retaliatory raid on Japan (USAF Photo)

Every mission needs a leader. This mission required only the best: famed aviator and aeronautical engineer James H. "Jimmy" Doolittle. A talented flyer and a charismatic leader, he was the perfect man for the job. Since the operation was secret, even President

18 | Denver and the Doolittle Raid

Roosevelt himself knew very little about the details. If word slipped out, things could go terribly wrong.

Once the plan was formed, the Army Air Corps began recruiting volunteers for the flight. Most of the volunteers weren't exactly sure what they were going to do, because those in charge were required to keep strict secrecy. They could only tell the men that the mission would be extremely dangerous. The recruits kept the secret and trained as they were told. Surprisingly, no one dropped out. However, one of the trainees, Staff Sergeant Jacob "Jake" DeShazer, later admitted to having second thoughts. As his superior asked for volunteers, giving them the option to decline, everyone said yes. Jake didn't want to be the only one to drop out. He, along with all the others, would soon find out what they were really getting themselves into.

One of the volunteers was a young airman named Denver V. Truelove from Lula, Georgia.

2

From Schoolboy to Soldier

Denver Vernon Truelove was born at home on April 10, 1919, in Clermont, Georgia. His parents were Clyde and Gertrude Truelove, and he had one older sister, Blanche.

Gertrude, Blanche, Clyde and one-year-old Denver Truelove

Mrs. Truelove taught her children Bible verses and encouraged them to memorize them. While working among rows of vegetables on the family farm, she would repeat the alphabet continually until her children knew the letters by heart. They also learned to count and write to 100. The family's only book was the New Testament of the Bible, and their mother used it to teach them basic reading skills.

While they lived in Clermont, they had to make a three-mile walk to school since no buses ran by their home in the country. However, the children valued the education they were getting. They enjoyed school and appreciated what their mother had already taught them.

Once, while Denver and his sister Blanche were making the long trek home from school, a bully jumped out from behind a tree and began calling Denver names. The bully punched him in the nose, making his nose start to bleed. Normally a gentle girl, Blanche's temper flared. Dashing over to her brother's rescue, she smacked the bully and he ran away. After that incident, the children were never bothered by him again. "I don't think I ever hit anyone else for the rest of my life," Blanche later shared. The children eventually moved to Lula, Georgia, and stayed with their aunt while they went to a nearby school.

In the 1930s, listening to the radio was becoming one of the nation's favorite pastimes. Families would gather around and listen to the few stations that existed in those days. President Roosevelt began his first term in 1933, and he used the radio to directly communicate with the people. Denver, who was almost fourteen at the time of Roosevelt's election, sat with Blanche and his parents, listening to the president's "fireside chats."

For farm families like the Trueloves, there was always plenty of work to do. As teenagers harvesting cotton and corn, Denver and Blanche would watch airplanes flying overhead. Denver dreamed of someday being able to fly in one.

Over the years, Denver grew up with a love for hard work and education. He and Blanche both attended Rabun Gap-Nacoochee Junior College in north Georgia.

Denver was handsome, immaculate, and a perfectionist. His classmates all knew that he took special care of his hair—and let no one mess with it. Once, while at a college chapel service, there was a guest speaker who would occasionally step down from the pulpit and ruffle someone's hair. Denver's classmates held their breath, barely concentrating on the speaker's message—would he touch Denver's hair? The speaker did not, however, and Denver's hair remained as perfect as ever.

Denver Truelove, age 19

Dr. Andrew Jackson Ritchie, the founder of the Rabun Gap school, did not drive. Since his wife Addie was almost always busy with secretarial duties and such, Ritchie would select a student to be his driver. Denver happened to be the lucky one that Dr. Ritchie picked, and, though he was teased by other classmates for being Ritchie's "pet", kept the job of driving his college mentor.

At Rabun Gap, Denver received his associate's degree before heading to the University of Georgia, where he planned to prepare to be a teacher of agriculture. He stayed at UGA two full quarters and was beginning his third term when he decided to enlist in the army in May of 1940. He volunteered for the Army Air Corps, the precursor of the U.S. Air Force.

Denver pursued training to be an army aircraft pilot at Tuscaloosa, Alabama, and Randolph Field, Texas, but in his own words he was simply "a little reckless" to be a pilot.

Denver beside a plane in Tuscaloosa, Alabama

While stationed in Denver, Colorado, he found a job that suited him just fine—that of a bombardier. His training as a bombardier then took him to Pendleton, Oregon.

During his college years, Denver had fallen in love with a beautiful young classmate at Rabun Gap. Although they got engaged while Denver was stationed at Pendleton, her dad made her return the engagement ring. Her father must not have wanted her to be brokenhearted, knowing that Denver might not return if he went off to war. Despite this, Denver still had many friends to whom he wrote letters during his service.

At the age of twenty-two, in 1942, he was informed of the United States' secret bombing mission. It would be incredibly dangerous, he was told. Along with almost a hundred other men, Denver volunteered. After all, he liked adventure and was eager for new experiences. Like everyone else who volunteered, Denver didn't know many details about the mission. He could only train and prepare for what he knew would be an extremely dangerous undertaking.

Denver's task was that of a bombardier, the man who dropped the bombs from a plane. At only about 5 feet 8 inches tall, Denver was the perfect one for the job, since his compact frame fit easily into the nose of the plane. He deemed his location to have the very best view in the B-25. However, many of the engineer/gunners, who rode in the glass-enclosed compartment on the top of the plane, insisted that they had the best seat.

The Mitchell B-25 Bomber

Once they arrived for training at Eglin Field in Valparaiso, Florida, all of the men wondered the same thing: what was their mission? They had been instructed not to talk about it among themselves, but many of them couldn't help wondering where their travels would take them. Could it be somewhere in the Pacific? Or perhaps bombing the Axis enemies in Europe?

Their training, led by Navy Lt. Henry L. "Hank" Miller, included taking off in their B-25's at the extremely short distance of 500 feet. Most of the pilots were used to a takeoff length of over 1,500 to 2,000 feet for a loaded bomber! The planes required many modifications to make them lighter and allow room for extra fuel tanks. The special, expensive Norden bombsight wouldn't work well at the low altitudes at which the planes would be flying during the mission. Instead, one of the Raiders, Captain C. Ross Greening, designed a "20-cent bombsight" that would work well at lower altitudes. This unusual bombsight cost only 20 cents to make, unlike the $10,000 secret Norden, which the U.S. did not want to see fall into enemy hands. Another plane alteration was the installation of two rear "guns"—broomsticks, painted black to look like .50 caliber machine guns. This was a clever tactic to make enemy planes think that they had more firepower than they actually did. The lower gun turret had to be removed, since it added extra weight and was complicated to operate. Also, there would be no need to fire it, since enemy planes wouldn't be able to fly low enough to be under the B-25's.

After weeks of training, all was finally ready. When the men were about to leave for McClellan Field in California, their families were allowed to visit them at Eglin. Denver's parents, his sister Blanche, her husband, and an aunt traveled from Georgia to say goodbye and wish him a safe mission.

Although Denver's family was sad to see him leave, they knew that the United States needed more men to win the war and brave ones to complete this mission. What none of them would have guessed was that it would become known as the famous Doolittle Tokyo Raid.

3

Aboard the Hornet

After leaving Eglin, the men flew across the country to McClellan Field in California. Final modifications to the planes were made before flying on to the naval base at Alameda, California. Their B-25's were loaded onto an aircraft carrier, the *U.S.S. Hornet*, which was waiting at the dock. After all their hard work in training, they were finally setting off.

The U.S.S. Hornet
(USN Photo)

Although the original plan called for more, only sixteen planes could be loaded aboard the *Hornet*, and Denver was to be on the fifth one. On each plane, there were five crew members: pilot, co-pilot, navigator, bombardier, and engineer/gunner. Eighty total men would comprise the final group for the mission.

As the ship passed under the Golden Gate Bridge on April 2, Denver knew that this mission, whatever it was, would be a big adventure. Setting out from San Francisco, the *Hornet* encountered fairly calm weather and enjoyable temperatures. Finally, after the ship was out at sea, the long-awaited secret was revealed to the men. The ship's loudspeaker blared, "This force is bound for Tokyo!" The men cheered and began singing their own version of a song from the Disney movie *Snow White*: "Heigh-ho! Heigh-ho! It's off to Tokyo we go! We'll bomb and blast and come back fast! Heigh-ho, heigh-ho, heigh-ho!" After bombing Japan, the plan was for the crews to land near Chuchow, China. The mission's leaders had arranged to have a radio beacon installed at a base in China, directing the planes to airstrips where they could land, refuel, and proceed to Chungking, China. There, they would leave their planes and return to the United States.

On April 10, 1942, as they were traveling closer to Japan, Denver celebrated his twenty-third birthday. In his diary, he wrote that he was "extremely happy to be alive and healthy."

The U.S.S. Hornet on its way to Japan
(Picture taken from the U.S.S. Enterprise, USN Photo)

Short tests were conducted frequently on the *Hornet* to prepare the men for the actual mission. An alarm would sound for them to man their planes, though they all knew it was only a drill. Once, obviously tired of the drills, Denver and another Raider, Ted Lawson, mischievously ignored the call to battle-stations and ate two hot, fresh blueberry pies that had just come out of the oven in the ship's galley. "The pie was perfect," Ted Lawson later wrote in his account of the mission, *Thirty Seconds over Tokyo*.

During the long trip to Japan, the *Hornet* was joined by an escort group led by Admiral William F. "Bull" Halsey, Jr., on the carrier U.S.S. *Enterprise*. While on the *Hornet*, the men were given instructions regarding their targets. Doolittle firmly commanded the men not to bomb the Emperor's Imperial Palace or civilian targets. They were to bomb military targets only, such as factories and storage facilities. Additionally, each separate crew had to know which city they were to bomb. Denver's plane was headed for the capital, Tokyo, though some planes would bomb other major Japanese cities. Gunners practiced their skills by shooting at kites flying from the back of the *Hornet* while the navigators pored over maps of Japan.

Originally, the raid was scheduled to take place on April 19, but that soon changed when a Japanese picket boat, the *Nitto Maru*, was spotted. The *Enterprise* ordered that it be sunk, although it had already radioed the Japanese military about seeing the loaded carrier at sea. Thankfully for the Raiders, the Japanese were having an air raid drill in Tokyo that day, and they did not pay much attention to the warning. This would cost them greatly, for they were unprepared for the surprise attack that was about to proceed.

Since they worried that the boat's radio call might have lost them the element of surprise, the Raiders would have to take off on April 18—a day earlier than planned—and much farther from Japan. They were still over 600 miles from Japan, and they had planned to take off at 400 miles away. Almost everyone was pondering the daunting question: would the Raiders have enough fuel to make it safely to China?

4
Off to Japan!

Denver's plane crew consisted of Lieutenant Eugene F. McGurl (navigator), Captain David M. "Davy" Jones (pilot), Lieutenant Denver V. Truelove (bombardier), Lieutenant Rodney R. "Hoss" Wilder (co-pilot), and Staff Sergeant Joseph W. Manske (engineer/gunner).

(L. to R.) Lt. Eugene McGurl, Capt. David Jones, Lt. Denver Truelove, Lt. Rodney Wilder, and Sgt. Joseph Manske
(USAF Photo)

At eight in the morning on April 18, Captain Marc "Pete" Mitscher, commanding officer of the *Hornet*, received this message from the *Enterprise* "LAUNCH PLANES. TO COL. DOOLITTLE AND GALLANT COMMAND GOOD LUCK AND GOD BLESS YOU." Once the message was received, the *Hornet*'s loudspeaker blared, "Army pilots, man your planes!" The crews of all sixteen bombers began hurriedly preparing for takeoff.

Doolittle Raid B-25's loaded on the deck of the U.S.S. Hornet
(Denver's plane is the one in the center that can be easily seen.)
(USAF Photo)

Quickly, they loaded a few more small fuel cans in the rear of the plane to be utilized later and checked the gas levels on their planes. Joseph Manske, the gunner/engineer on Denver's plane, and some sailors from the *Hornet* had fueled plane #5, but one leaky gas tank was still thirty gallons short. Manske tried to fill the tank, but it was nearly time to take off. Thankfully, C. Ross Greening, the creator of the 20-cent bombsight, donated a few of his five-gallon cans to Captain Jones. Still, because of the early takeoff, it was evident that it would not be an easy feat for the Raiders to make it all the way to free China after bombing their target cities: Nagoya, Osaka, Kobe, Yokohama, and, of course, Tokyo.

An Army Air Force B-25 bomber takes off from USS Hornet (CV-8) at the start of the raid, 18 April 1942.
(USN Photo)

Taking off from the *Hornet*'s flight deck was difficult because of the limited amount of space. However, plane #1, with Jimmy Doolittle at the controls and co-pilot Dick Cole at his side, zoomed off into the distance, making a remarkable takeoff at only 463 feet. One by one, the planes soared off the deck of the carrier. Soon Denver's plane was up. According to Davy Jones, Denver's pilot, the takeoff of plane #5 was made without difficulty, and they took off from the *Hornet* at 8:37 a.m.

As Japan still lay far in the distance, the engineer/gunner, Joe Manske, called Captain Jones on the intercom.

"Sir," Manske said urgently, "We don't have enough gas!"

"That's right!" Davy Jones replied, and then hung up with a click. There was nothing they could do about their decreasing fuel; they could only hope for a miracle or prepare for a water landing.

As Denver's plane approached the coast of Japan, Captain Jones steered the plane lower. When the thick clouds cleared out, they realized they were slightly off course, so Jones turned the plane northward as they made their way swiftly along, approaching the Tokyo coastline. Denver remarked, "We flew close to the water and the biggest thrill I got was when we approached the enemy island. Buildings suddenly loomed up from the ocean and the plane shot up to a higher altitude for bombing."

Coastline of Japan; photo taken from a Doolittle Raid plane (USAF Photo)

As they flew over Tokyo Bay, Captain Jones notified Denver that it was almost time to drop the bombs. Denver prepared his instruments, including the 20-cent bombsight, and gave instructions to Captain Jones via the intercom as to what direction he should head. Denver knew that they were now in the heart of enemy territory, but there was no time for fear. "I hoped I could perform the duty I was sent to carry out," Denver later wrote. "You forget everything but your job in a case like that."

As the plane neared the target, Denver dropped the first bomb. It made a direct hit on a nearby oil storage tank, which exploded in a blaze. The second bomb also directly hit its target, blasting a storage plant, and the third bomb hit a factory, spreading out perfectly over its intended mark.

The B-25 was approaching its last target, so Denver prepared to drop the final bomb—an incendiary. When Davy Jones suddenly increased the plane's speed to escape enemy anti-aircraft fire, the fourth and final bomb only scraped the edge of its target. Always a perfectionist, missing the last target disappointed Denver, but he knew that the first part of their mission was over. Now Captain Jones, co-pilot "Hoss" Wilder, and the navigator "Gene" McGurl had to fly and navigate the plane to safety in China. Once in China, they expected to receive the radio beacon that would direct them to the Chinese airfield where they could land.

As soon as the plane reached the water again, they reduced their speed to save fuel. When they left the coastline of Japan and entered the China Sea, the weather became so fierce that they could hardly see through the torrent of wind and rain. However, a strong tailwind pushed the dying planes from Japan on to China. They could barely make out the coastline in the distance. However, a landing there would be impossible because of the darkness, the stormy weather, and the fact that the Japanese had occupied that portion of China. Gliding through the misty darkness, they reached the Chinese coastline at 8:10 p.m. ship time. It had been almost twelve hours since they took off from the *Hornet*.

Davy Jones knew that they were somewhere near the Chinese city of Chuchow (sometimes called Chuhsien), but the air fields could not be seen, and there were no radio signals. Parachuting from the plane was now their only option.

"[Captain Jones] called me over [the] interphone to come out of the nose and prepare to bail out…Sgt. Manske, the rear gunner, and I were to jump…as near together as possible," Denver recalled. Preparing to jump, the crew opened the two escape hatches and donned their chutes. It was time to drop into the enveloping darkness below. The only light came from occasional flashes of lightning around them.

Denver and Joe Manske parachuted together through the escape hatches: Denver through the front one and Joe through the rear hatch. Following behind them was Gene McGurl and then Lieutenant Wilder. Captain Jones was the last to jump. They hated to leave the plane, but it was their only way of survival. Soon, the plane would simply run out of gas and crash.

Denver sailed downward into the night sky, not knowing what lay below. His buddy, Joe, had decided to stuff twelve Baby Ruth candy bars into his flight jacket. However, by the time Joe reached the ground, all he had left was the wrappers! The force of the opening parachute had ripped the candy bars out.

Denver and Joe landed on a mountain nearby. Their parachutes were caught in a tree, but Denver was able to free himself and Sergeant Manske. The tree tore Manske's parachute to shreds, so they used Denver's parachute to protect them from the downpour of rain. It was a restless night, and, as they drifted off to sleep, both men wondered how they would get to their next stop—Chuchow.

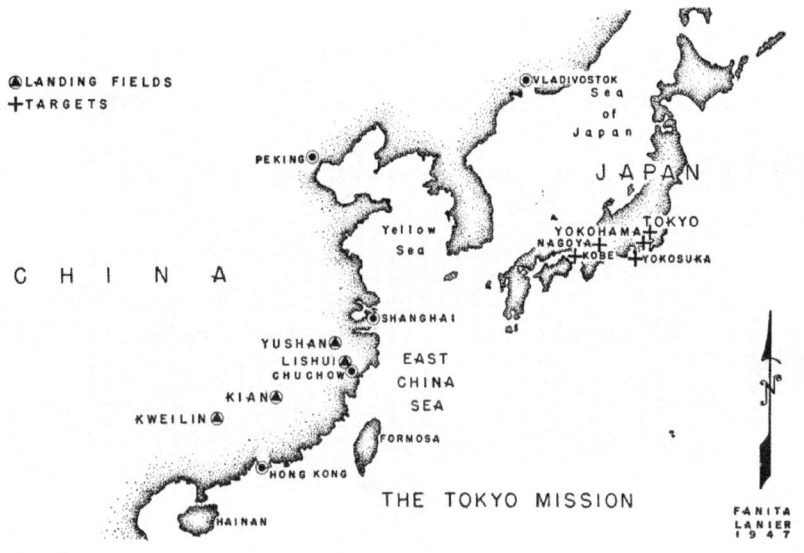

This map shows some of the major cities of the Doolittle Raid. Notice Tokyo (where Denver bombed) and Chuchow (plane #5's bail-out location). Although several Chinese landing fields are noted, none were used due to the absent radio beacons. (USAF Map)

"April 18th [1942] was a very long, important day: our first attack on the Japanese, and the first bomb ever dropped on Tokyo," Denver would write in his diary. The Japanese emperor Hirohito had told his people that he was a god, and they believed that their country could never be bombed or attacked. They thought they were invincible. The Doolittle Raid proved them wrong—and provided a turning point in morale for the Allies in World War II. After the raid, the fortunes of the Japanese were gradually reversed. They would never again expand their empire, beginning their retreat back to the home islands. They withdrew some of their forces to protect their homeland from more air attacks, and this began to pave the way for the Allies' eventual victory in September 1945.

Doolittle's Tokyo Raid truly was a turning point in the Pacific war. It would prove to be a pivotal mission that changed the course of history.

5

Farther into China

The next day, Denver and Joe Manske woke up to see the bright China sun shining over them. Thankfully, neither of the men was hurt besides a few scrapes and bruises. Both of them knew that the next step was to get to Chuchow…but how?

Denver and Joe walked to the nearest Chinese village, but no one there could speak English. Since there was no way to communicate with the people of this village, they continued walking to the next town, where they found an English-speaking school teacher who helped them travel farther toward their destination. They reached a city where they were taken in by three ladies from the China Inland Mission.

Although they were exhausted from their journey, Denver and Joe were the first Raiders to reach Chuchow, arriving at three p.m. on April 19. Soon after they arrived, Davy Jones phoned Denver to tell him that he had also arrived in Chuchow. Although Denver was tired, he was pleased to hear his pilot's voice.

The next day, however, the Japanese led bombing raids over the Chuchow (Chuhsien) area. Several crews, including crew #5, were kept in air raid shelters due to the constant Japanese attacks.

Doolittle Raiders and Chinese helpers hide out near an air raid shelter. Denver is on the back row, far left. (USAF Photo)

Not all the crews had fared as well as Denver's. Plane #7, called "The Ruptured Duck," crash-landed near the coast while trying to make a beach landing. The pilot, Ted Lawson, who shared blueberry pies with Denver aboard the *Hornet*, had been severely injured along with several of his crewmembers. The four injured men in Lawson's crew were helped by their engineer/gunner, 20-year-old David Thatcher, one of the youngest men on the raid. Lawson said, "I don't know what we would have done without Thatcher." Although Lawson lived, he had to have his left leg amputated by Lieutenant T. Robert "Doc" White of plane #15, a medical doctor who had volunteered to go on the raid as a gunner. Both Thatcher and "Doc" White were awarded the Silver Star for aiding the injured crew.

"The Chinese people are very good at heart," Denver said of those who assisted them. Eventually, with the help of the kind Chinese citizens, Denver and many other Raiders were able to go by foot, bus, and train to Hengyang. There, an American C-47 plane flew them to Chungking, China, and they arrived on the evening of April 29. Now that they had made it to safety, the Raiders were treated to the hospitality of Madame May Ling Soong Chiang of China, the wife of Generalissimo Chiang Kai-Shek. She awarded them Chinese Air Force medals and held a huge banquet for them before they left China. Denver enjoyed the meal, especially the ice cream and lemon pie they had for dessert!

Madame Chiang was a wonderful hostess and particularly liked Denver's last name because it sounded like "true love." She had been educated at a preparatory school in Georgia, as well as Wellesley College in Massachusetts. Her time in America helped her to learn English fluently, and, like Denver, she had a Southern accent, helping her to connect with the Americans. Before they left, each Raider was given a copy of a letter that Madame Chiang had written, thanking them for their bravery. The letter read:

> To the Valiant American Airmen who bombed Japan:
>
> It is with mixed feelings that I write these words. I have looked forward to the pleasure of seeing you for you represent America where I have so many friends, and to tell you what your gallant exploit in braving unknown dangers to bring war to Japan has meant to my people.
>
> We have for five years suffered the inhumanities and barbarities of the Japanese military, not only on land and sea, but also from the skies. The lion heart of your great President must have throbbed with grief at the distress of millions of my countrymen who have endured uncomplainingly but none the less painfully the agonies of remorseless Japanese aggression. I feel certain that this must have largely influenced his decision to send you on a mission which would put an end to inhuman warfare. The entire Chinese people are grateful to you and to him for your brave deeds. I venture to think that you have even helped to lay the myriad ghosts

of cities, villages, men, women and children who have been the innocent victims of Japanese bombs.

I was glad of the opportunity to thank you on behalf of my compatriots. The Generalissimo and I both were happy to see you. We hope for days to come when you will revisit China in happier circumstances. Our Chinese people will always welcome you with friendship and admiration.

Meanwhile may all be well with you. May you continue to vindicate freedom and justice so that by your efforts a happier and more unselfish world society will evolve when victory is ours.

May Ling Soong Chiang

In the following days, Madame Chiang's people would be brutally attacked and harassed by the Japanese for helping the Americans. Hundreds of thousands would lose their lives as the angry Japanese military unleashed their fury upon the Chinese. But through it all, the Chinese would still persevere in gratefulness for what the Doolittle Raiders had done.

The small group of men had accomplished what was supposedly impossible: bombing Japan, the "empire of the rising sun."

HEADQUARTERS OF THE GENERALISSIMO
CHINA

Chungking, Szechuan
1 May, 1942

To the Valiant American Airmen who bombed Japan:

    It is with mixed feelings that I write these words. I have looked forward to the pleasure of seeing you for you represent America where I have so many friends, and to tell you what your gallant exploit in braving unknown dangers to bring war to Japan has meant to my people.

    We have for five years suffered the inhumanities and barbarities of the Japanese military, not only on land and sea, but also from the skies. The lion heart of your great President must have throbbed with grief at the distress of millions of my countrymen who have endured uncomplainingly but none the less painfully the agonies of remorseless Japanese aggression. I feel certain that this must have largely influenced his decision to send you on a mission which would put an end to inhuman warfare. The entire Chinese people are grateful to you and to him for your brave deeds. I venture to think that you have even helped to lay the myriad ghosts of cities, villages, men, women and children, who have been the innocent victims of Japanese bombs.

    I was glad of the opportunity to thank you on behalf of my compatriots. The Generalissimo and I both were happy to see you. We hope for days to come when you will revisit China in happier circumstances. Our Chinese people will always welcome you with friendship and admiration.

    Meanwhile may all be well with you. May you continue to vindicate freedom and justice so that by your efforts a happier and more unselfish world society will evolve when victory is ours.

Second Lieutenant
    Denver V. Truelove

May-ling Soong Chiang

Denver's Letter from Madame Chiang Kai-Shek

6

Home at Last

Denver then traveled to India after being in Chungking. It had been two years since he signed into the army. "A proud cadet I was! Eager for experiences. Little did I dream of this, though," he remarked in his diary. Denver then traveled through Pakistan before flying to Egypt. While in Egypt, he purchased some ivory, crossed over the Nile River on a bridge, observed the pyramids at Giza, and saw the famous Great Sphinx.

After his time in Egypt, Denver and some of the other Raiders traveled to Nigeria. There, they were delayed for a while, simply waiting for transportation. Denver remarked that a train he was on traveled through a dust storm, and he "ate dust" the whole trip. After this, they flew to Trinidad, where they happened to see the King of Greece.

Traveling around the world was interesting, but Denver longed to be home at last—back in his own country and his hometown of Lula, Georgia. He missed his family and was excited when, on June 10, 1942, the group of Raiders arrived in Miami, Florida.

Some of the Doolittle Raiders posing for a picture in Washington, D.C. Left to Right: Davenport, Hilger, Pound, Greening, Bower, White, Macia, Smith, Truelove (USAF Photo)

Back in America, the Raiders received a heroes' welcome. In Washington, D.C., Denver received the Distinguished Flying Cross for his participation in the courageous mission.

After losing all his planes, Jimmy Doolittle said he expected to be court-martialed when he arrived home. He received a treatment quite different from what he expected: the Medal of Honor. When President Franklin Roosevelt awarded him the Medal of Honor for his bravery, Doolittle firmly announced that the medal was for every man who helped in the raid. After being given the medal, Doolittle announced, "I will spend the rest of my life trying to earn it."

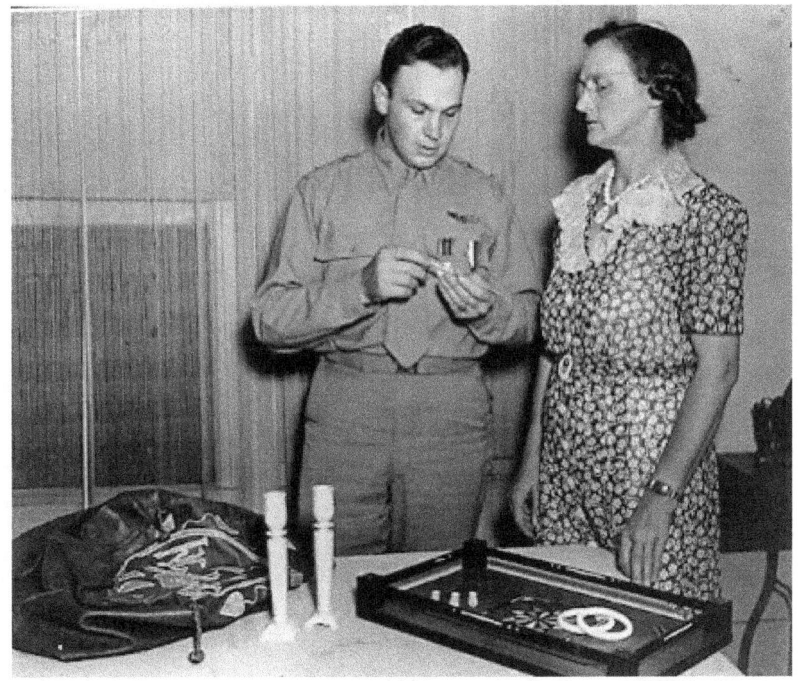

Denver shows his mother, Gertrude Truelove, some of the treasures he collected while traveling on the way home from the Doolittle Raid.

After he received the Distinguished Flying Cross, Denver returned to his hometown of Lula, Georgia. His family and the townsfolk greeted him cheerfully. Denver brought home many gifts from Africa, including ivory candlesticks and intricate jewelry for his mother and sister.

Denver with his cousins, Lurlene & Gwendolyn Smelley (USASC Photo)

While he was home, Denver was on a mission to promote the sale of war bonds, because he wanted to help the American cause in any way he could. War bonds would help fund the war and give Americans one more reason to hope. According to the *Atlanta*

Constitution, Denver outsold the famous Hollywood actress Dorothy Lamour when he sold $70,000 worth of bonds.

Denver (center) drinks a Coca-Cola as he talks to some new army recruits at a July 4, 1943, Independence Day celebration

Because Denver was such a successful war bond promoter, he became an even greater hero on the home front. The fame of the Doolittle Raiders spread, and Denver was even mentioned in a Helena, Montana newspaper, *The Helena Independent*! Everyone admired him, and a local newspaper described him as "handsomer than any of his pictures indicate, has brown hair, ruddy cheeks, brown eyes and, of all things—two dimples." Parades and big celebrations were held in honor of this new hero.

While Denver and most of the other Raiders had arrived home safely, a few had not. One of the planes, piloted by Edward "Ski" York and co-piloted by Robert Emmens, was extremely low on fuel because of an engine problem. They diverted their plane to Russia where they were interned by the Soviets for thirteen months before making a daring escape into Iran, then known as Persia.

One crew crash-landed and another bailed out in Japanese-occupied China, and the eight men who survived were captured. Sadly, the Japanese executed three of the Raiders and tortured the rest in prison camps. One of them died of malnutrition. The remaining four captured Raiders had to survive solitary confinement and malnourishment as Japanese POW's (Prisoners of War). Only the war's end would reveal their fate.

7

Denver's Final Mission

The Doolittle Raid had ultimately been a success. Denver had promoted the sale of thousands of dollars in war bonds and was a great hero. Now he continued his service in the Army Air Corps.

(USASC Photo)

Denver was sent to Europe for a short time. He worked in England for only a month before he was transferred to North Africa. From there, the U.S. was strategically planning to bomb Italy, one of the Axis enemies. In a letter home, Denver wrote, "When I do not fly, I check others out and in. Some do not return. I have been around the world. Our country is the best, and I am willing to die for our USA."

It was now September 1942, and Denver, a member of the 310th Bomb Group, 428th Squadron, was promoted to the rank of captain. He was working alongside his good friend, William M. "Bill" Bower, the former pilot of crew #12 in the raid on Japan. The two men had a genuine friendship and enjoyed each other's company.

On April 5, 1943, Denver, Bill, and many others were sent on a bombing mission to Italy. After completing their mission, the planes were flying back to their base in North Africa. However, during their mission, Denver's plane had been damaged by enemy fire over Italy. A plane piloted by one of Bill Bower's friends was about half an hour behind Denver's plane as they returned from their mission. During stormy weather over the Mediterranean Sea, the crew spotted the wreckage of Denver's plane in the ocean, sinking slowly.

There are conflicting views on what happened next. According to Bill, Denver had managed to crawl out of the plane onto the wing and waved at the plane passing overhead. When a rescue plane finally arrived at the scene, Denver was gone.

However, other sources relate that Denver was immediately knocked unconscious as his plane hit the ocean waves, and no one could help him in the stormy seas. To this day, no one knows for certain what happened to him, although the pilot and a few other crewmembers on his plane were rescued. Denver was listed as MIA (Missing In Action), and he was never found.

This incident happened on April 5, 1943, only five days before Denver's twenty-fourth birthday.

Denver's family mourned his loss; it was a great blow. Blanche, his sister, silently grieved, treasuring each memory she had of him. Even amidst the sadness of death, there was much to be proud of in Denver's life.

Denver did many things during World War II. Bravely, he took part in the Doolittle Tokyo Raid, although it was a secret mission that he knew could have cost him his life. After dropping bombs on Japan in the raid, he was a decorated hero. Also, he promoted war bonds and helped to raise thousands of dollars for the American cause.

Some of Denver's medals left to right: Air Medal with Oak Leaf Cluster, Distinguished Flying Cross, Purple Heart, and Chinese Air Force Medal

He received numerous medals, among them the Distinguished Flying Cross, Purple Heart, Air Medal with Three Oak Leaf Cluster, American Campaign Medal, Defense Medal, Foreign Service Medal, and the Chinese Air Force Medal.

Denver's name is listed on the Tablets of the Missing, North Africa American Cemetery, Carthage, Tunisia, as TRUELOVE DENVER V.

A section of the Tablets of the Missing
(American Battle Monuments Commission)

The war would rage on for two more years, until August, 1945. Then, when the United States dropped atomic bombs on the Japanese cities of Hiroshima and Nagasaki, Japan finally surrendered to the Allies. The U.S. had triumphed in the war that had claimed Denver's life. The four surviving Doolittle Raider POW's—Robert Hite, George Barr, Jacob DeShazer and Chase Nielsen—who had been held as prisoners by the Japanese, were released soon after the victory. One of these men, Jacob DeShazer, returned as a Christian missionary to the country where, only a few years before, he had been held captive for forty months—a testimony to the power of forgiveness.

Shortly after the Japanese surrendered, Denver's sister, Blanche, gave birth to her first child, a son, whom she named Denver in memory of her brother. Many years later, Colonel Bill Bower would bring Blanche a copy of Colonel Carroll V. Glines' book, *Doolittle's Tokyo Raiders*, with this inscription in it:

> To Blanche Truelove Bowen,
>
> In remembrance of your brother and my wartime comrade, friend—Denver. The survivors of this action each year raise their goblets in toast to those who have gone before. Each has a special place in our memory.
>
> Bill Bower

Denver Truelove was truly a valiant war hero and a great young man. He loved his country enough to give his life so that others could have freedom.

Capt. Denver Vernon Truelove
1919-1943

8

A Continuing Legacy

Over half a century after Denver's death, a special monument was erected in honor of his life and legacy. In 2010, this stone memorial was placed in his hometown of Lula, Georgia.

Gathering at the new Veterans Memorial Park in Lula, a large group commemorated Denver's contribution to their country. Blanche Truelove Bowen, Denver's sister, now a 93 year old great-grandmother, attended the memorial ceremony. The stone memorial stands in the center of Lula, right by the railroad tracks. It serves as a proud reminder of a young Georgian—and American—who was willing to give his life to keep his beloved country free.

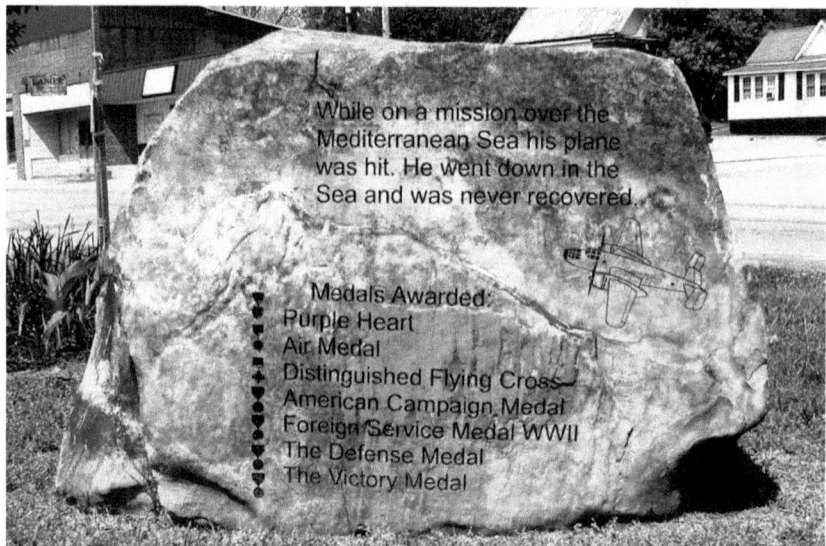

This memorial, like other memorials to those who have served this country, continues to remind us what true courage is.

In 2008, just a couple of years prior to the monument's creation, the Gwinnett County Veterans Memorial Museum in Lawrenceville, Georgia, creat-ed a special exhibit for Denver Truelove and the Doolittle Tokyo Raid. It includes photographs, facts, and a model of the U.S.S. *Hornet*, so that those who have never heard of the raid can be enlightened and amazed. Now all who visit the museum will learn of a new hero and his daring mission: Denver and the Doolittle Raid.

※

There is another chapter in the story of the Doolittle Raid—one that has continued year after year. On the U.S.S. *Hornet*, before the raid, Jimmy Doolittle had promised to throw his men "a party." In keeping with his word, the Doolittle Raiders held the promised party in December of 1945 in Miami, Florida. Here they were up until all hours of the morning at the hotel pool. The manager complained, but admitted that they had "earned it." During the reunion, they sent this letter, signed by forty-six of the original Raiders, to Blanche:

> In Remembrance: Denver V. Truelove
>
> We, the comrades of D. V. Truelove send you this remembrance, upon the occasion of the first reunion of the original Tokyo raid flyers, gathered here at Miami, Florida, on the 15th of December 1945.
>
> Denny is here with us—in spirit—just as he is with you today. He will ever be with us through the years to come.
>
> In his memory and that of his lost comrades this gathering of his buddies who knew him and loved him because of the many sterling qualities he possessed and for the part he played in the service of his country.

Since this first party was great fun for the men, they voted to have one each year. The parties grew and became known as the "Doolittle Raider Reunions." They were held in various cities across the U.S., changing places every year.

The Doolittle Raiders' goblet case, containing the eighty silver goblets that were presented to them by the city of Tucson, Arizona

The reunions are both joyful and poignant. At the 1959 reunion in Tucson, Arizona, the Raiders were presented with eighty silver goblets with the names of the Doolittle Raiders inscribed on them. While a Raider is still living, his goblet is turned upwards. When he has passed away, the goblet is turned over, and his remaining comrades have a toast in their own goblets. Doolittle himself decided that, when only two of the Raiders were left, they would share one final toast to the other seventy-eight men. In 2013, with only four Raiders remaining, they chose to move ahead and hold that last toasting ceremony. Three of the Raiders were able to attend—Richard Cole, David Thatcher, and Edward Saylor—and so Doolittle's wish was fulfilled.

The Doolittle Raiders ultimately received the greatest national honor for their service and sacrifice. In 2015, seventy-three years after the raid, the eighty airmen were finally awarded the Congressional Gold Medal. This award truly sealed their rightful place in history as American heroes.

A bronze replica of the Doolittle Raiders' intricate Congressional Gold Medal

The Doolittle Tokyo Raiders' Congressional Gold Medal came to stay at the National Museum of the Air Force, where it stands along with the silver goblets—an unending reminder of the simple courage of eighty brave men.

Denver's goblet, though now long inverted, still stands along with the others. May his legacy continue to weave its way down through multiple generations, so that all will remember the daring Doolittle Raid.

Author's Notes

Everything included in this book is true to the best of my knowledge and research. Denver Truelove was my great-great-uncle and served under Jimmy Doolittle in the 1942 raid on Japan.

The Doolittle Raiders' Crest
(Used with permission of the Doolittle Tokyo Raiders Association, Inc.)

The motto on the Doolittle Raider's crest is "Toujours au danger," which is French for "Ever into danger." The seven Maltese crosses, standing for the seven World War I campaigns, represent the 17th Bombardment Group, from which the Raid crews volunteered. (Ironically, yet sadly, seven of the Doolittle Raiders died as a direct result of the raid: Faktor, Dieter, Fitzmaurice, Farrow, Spatz, Hallmark, and Meder.) The 34th Squadron is represented by the Thunderbird, in the circle, top right. The 95th Squadron, which Denver was in, is represented by the kicking mule, bottom right. The 37th Squadron is represented by the tiger, bottom left, and the 89th Reconnaissance Squadron is represented by the winged helmet. Over the Maltese crosses, a Mitchell B-25 bomber flies.

The stone memorial mentioned in chapter eight is located in Lula, Georgia, at the corner of Athens Street and Main Street by the railroad tracks. The memorial is part of a Veterans Memorial Park, which, opposite the stone monument, has a brick wall with veterans' names inscribed on it. The first one is Capt D Truelove. Also, the Gwinnett County Veterans Memorial Museum in Lawrenceville, Georgia, contains the exhibit for Denver and the Doolittle Raiders mentioned in the final chapter of this book.

Part of the research for this book was completed by my attendance at the sixty-ninth Doolittle Raider reunion in Omaha, Nebraska. I was privileged to be able to meet all five Raiders who were living at that time (Richard "Dick" Cole, David Thatcher, Thomas "Tom" Griffin, Edward "Ed" Saylor, and Robert "Bob" Hite), plus Carroll V. Glines, the official Doolittle Raid historian. Denver's dear friend, Bill Bower, had died just a few months previously, but I had the privilege of meeting his son and daughters.

For anyone who wants to learn more about the Doolittle Raid, I would suggest Carroll V. Glines's books including *Doolittle's Tokyo Raiders, The Doolittle Raid,* and *Four Came Home.* Also, I recommend Stan Cohen's pictorial book *Destination: Tokyo.* Of course, a must-read for any Doolittle Raid fan is the timeless classic *Thirty Seconds Over Tokyo* by Raider Ted Lawson, which was subsequently made into the 1944 movie of the same title.

This book has truly taken me on a journey. At the time of this third edition, I have attended the 69th, 70th, and 71st reunions, as well as the final toast and the Congressional Gold Medal ceremony. The more time I have spent with the Raiders and their families, the more pieces I find to Denver's story.

Writing about Denver was enjoyable, interesting, and challenging. It has taken me to new places that I'd never been and introduced me to new people I'd never met. I hope this account will bring the same to you.

Sincerely,

Bo Burnette
Joshua 1:9—"Be strong and courageous."

Appendix:
Doolittle Raid Crews

Crew #1

(Plane 40-2344). Left to right: Lt. Henry A. Potter (navigator), Lt. Col. James H. Doolittle (pilot), S/Sgt. Fred A. Braemer (bombardier), Lt. Richard E. Cole (co-pilot), S/Sgt. Paul J Leonard (engineer-gunner).

Sgt. Paul Leonard was killed in Algeria on January 5, 1943.

Crew #2

(Plane 40-2292). Left to right: Lt Carl R. Wildner (navigator), Lt. Travis Hoover (pilot), Lt. Richard E. Miller (bombardier), Lt. William N. Fitzhugh (co-pilot), Sgt. Douglas V. Radney (engineer-gunner).

Lt. Richard Miller died January 22, 1943, over North Africa.

Appendix: Doolittle Raid Crews | 79

Crew #3

(Plane 40-2270). Left to right: Lt. Charles J. Ozuk (navigator), Lt. Robert M. Gray (pilot), Sgt. Aden E. Jones (bombardier), Lt. Jacob E. Manch (co-pilot), Cpl. Leland D. Faktor (engineer-gunner).

Cpl. Leland Faktor was killed bailing out over China.

Lt. Robert Gray was killed on October 18, 1942, on a mission near Assum, India.

Crew #4

(Plane 40-2282). Left to right: Lt. Harry C. McCool (navigator), Cpl. Bert M. Jordan (gunner), Lt. Everett W. Holstrom (pilot), Sgt. Robert J. Stephens (bombardier), and Lt. Lucian N. Youngblood (co-pilot).

Crew #5

(Plane 40-2283). Left to right: Lt. Eugene F. McGurl (navigator), Capt. David M. Jones (pilot), Lt Denver V. Truelove (bombardier), Lt. Rodney R. Wilder (co-pilot), and Sgt. Joseph W. Manske (engineer-gunner).

Lt. Eugene McGurl (KIA/MIA) died in a plane crash after bombing Burma on June 3, 1942.

Lt. Denver Truelove (KIA/MIA) was killed after enemy fire hit his plane near Sicily on April 5, 1943.

Crew #6

(Plane 40-2298). Left to right: Lt. Col. Chase Jay Nielsen (navigator), Lt. Dean E. Hallmark (pilot), Sgt. Donald E. Fitzmaurice (engineer-gunner), Lt. Robert J. Meder (co-pilot), Sgt. William J Dieter (bombardier).

This crew crashed in the water near Japanese-occupied China. William Dieter and Donald Fitzmaurice were killed in the crash, and the rest were captured by the Japanese. Dean Hallmark was executed, and Bob Meder died of dysentery and malnutrition in Japanese prison camps. Chase Nielsen alone survived the forty months of captivity and torture.

Appendix: Doolittle Raid Crews | 83

Crew #7

(Plane 40-2261). Left to right: Lt. Charles L McClure (navigator), Lt. Ted W. Lawson (pilot), Lt. Robert S. Clever (bombardier), Lt. Dean Davenport (co-pilot), Sgt. David J. Thatcher (engineer-gunner).

Lt. Robert Clever was killed in a plane crash near Versailles, Ohio, on November 20, 1942.

Crew #8

(Plane 40-2242). Left to right: Lt. Nolan A. Herndon (navigator-bombardier), Capt. Edward J. York (pilot), S/Sgt. Theodore H. Laban (engineer), Lt. Robert G. Emmens (co-pilot), and Sgt. David W. Pohl (gunner).

This crew landed in Vladivostok, Russia, and was interned for thirteen months before they made a daring escape to Persia (modern day Iran).

Crew #9

(Plane 40-2303). Left to right: Lt. Thomas C. Griffin (navigator), Lt. Harold F. Watson (pilot), T/Sgt. Eldred V. Scott (engineer-gunner), Lt. James N. Parker, Jr. (co-pilot), and Sgt. Wayne M. Bissell (bombardier).

Crew #10

(Plane 40-2250). Left to right: Lt. Horace E. Crouch (navigator/bombardier), Lt. Richard O. Joyce (pilot), unidentified gunner, who was replaced at the last minute by S/Sgt. Edwin W. Horton, Jr. (pictured in inset), Lt J. Royden Stork (co-pilot), Sgt. George F. Larkin, Jr. (flight engineer).

S/Sgt. George Larkin, Jr. was killed on October 18, 1942, on a mission near Assum, India.

Crew #11

(Plane 40-2249). Left to right: Lt. Frank A Kappeler (navigator), Capt. C. Ross Greening (pilot), Sgt. Melvin J. Gardner (engineer-gunner), Lt. Kenneth E. Reddy (co-pilot), S/Sgt. William L. Birch (bombardier).

S/Sgt. Melvin Gardner died from a plane crash on June 3, 1942, after bombing a target in Burma.

Lt. Kenneth Reddy was killed in a plane crash on September 3, 1942, near Little Rock, Arkansas.

Crew #12

(Plane 40-2278). Left to right: Lt. William R. Pound, Jr. (navigator), Lt. William M. Bower (pilot), S/Sgt. Omer A. Duquette (engineer-gunner), Lt Thadd H. Blanton (co-pilot), T/Sgt. Waldo J. Bither (bombardier).

S/Sgt. Omer Duquette died from a plane crash on June 3, 1942, after bombing a target in Burma.

Appendix: Doolittle Raid Crews | 89

Crew #13

(Plane 40-2247). Left to right: Lt. Clayton J. Campbell (navigator), Lt. Edgar E. McElroy (pilot), Sgt. Adam R. Williams (engineer-gunner), Lt. Richard A. Knobloch (co-pilot), Sgt. Robert C. Bourgeois (bombardier).

Crew #14

(Plane 40-2297). Left to right: Lt. James H Macia, Jr. (navigator-bombardier), Maj. John A Hilger (pilot), S/Sgt. Jacob Eierman (engineer), Lt. Jack A. Sims (co-pilot), M/Sgt. Edwin V. Bain (gunner).

M/Sgt. Edwin Bain (KIA/MIA) died on July 19, 1942 in a plane crash after the first raid over Rome, Italy.

Appendix: Doolittle Raid Crews | 91

Crew #15

(Plane 40-2267). Left to right: Lt. Howard A Sessler (navigator-bombardier), Lt. Donald G. Smith (pilot), Lt. (Dr.) Thomas R. White (gunner), Lt. Griffith P. Williams (co-pilot), and Sgt. Edward J. Saylor (engineer).

Lt. Don Smith was killed in Western Europe as a result of crash injuries on November 12, 1942.

Crew #16

(Plane 40-2268). Left to right: Lt. George Barr (navigator), Lt. William G. Farrow (pilot), Sgt. Harold A. Spatz (engineer-gunner), Lt. Robert L. Hite (co-pilot), and Cpl. Jacob DeShazer (bombardier).

This crew bailed out in Japanese-occupied China and was captured. The Japanese executed Harold Spatz and Will Farrow, but Jake DeShazer, Bob Hite, and George Barr survived forty months in prison camps.

Bibliography

Ambrose, Stephen E. *The Good Fight: How World War II Was Won.* New York, NY: Atheneum Books, 2001.

Benge, Janet & Geoff. *Jacob DeShazer: Forgive Your Enemies.* Seattle, WA: YWAM Publishing, 2009.

Cohen, Stan. *Destination Tokyo.* Missoula, MT: Pictorial Histories Publishing, 1983.

Dean, Austin F. "Lula To Hold Big Celebration Tomorrow in Honor of Truelove." *The Atlanta Constitution,* July 12, 1942.

Doolittle, James H. "Jimmy" with Carroll V. Glines. *I Could Never Be So Lucky Again.* New York: Bantam Books, 1991.

Donovan, Sandy. *Madame Chiang Kai-Shek: Face of Modern China.* Mankato, MN: Compass Point Books, 2007.

Drez, Ronald J. *Twenty-five Yards of War: The Extraordinary Courage of Ordinary Men in World War II.* New York: Hyperion, 2001.

Evans, Betty Jo. "This Lula Man Flew in the Legendary Raid on Tokyo". *Lula,* 2003.

Gill, Jeff. "Lula creates memorial for WWII veteran, native son." *The Gainesville Times* (Gainesville, GA), April 13, 2010.

Glines, Carroll V. *Doolittle's Tokyo Raiders.* New York: Van Nostrand Reinhold Publishing, 1964.

_____. *The Doolittle Raid: America's daring first strike against Japan.* New York: Orion Books, 1988.

_____. *Four Came Home.* New York: Van Nostrand Reinhold Publishing, 1981.

———. *James H. "Jimmy" Doolittle: Master of the Calculated Risk.* Missoula, MT: Pictorial Histories Publishing, 2002.

Goldstein, Donald M. & Carol Aiko DeShazer Dixon. *Return of the Raider: A Doolittle Raider's Story of War and Forgiveness.* Lake Mary, FL: Creation House, 2010.

Greening, Col. C. Ross. *Not as Briefed: From the Doolittle Raid to a German Stalag.* Pullman, WA: Washington State University Press, 2001.

Hoppes, Jonna Doolittle. *Calculated Risk: The Extraordinary Life of Jimmy Doolittle—Aviation Pioneer and World War II Hero.* Santa Monica Press, 2005.

Jones, David M. Diary. March 31-June 16, 1942.

Lawson, Ted W. *Thirty Seconds over Tokyo.* New York: Simon & Schuster, 2002.

Thirty Seconds Over Tokyo. Directed by Mervyn LeRoy. 1944. Burbank, CA: Warner Home Video, 2007. DVD.

Jimmy Doolittle: An American Hero. Directed by David Hoffman. 1989. Varied Directions, 2005. DVD.

Missions That Changed the War: The Doolittle Raid. With Gary Sinise. 2010. Discovery Network/The Military Channel, 2010. Video on Demand.

Merrill, James M. *Target Tokyo.* Rand McNally, 1964.

Osborne, Jeanne. "Jap Bombing Hero 'Available'---Hasn't Any Special Sweetheart." *The Atlanta Constitution,* July 4, 1942.

Schultz, Duane. *The Doolittle Raid.* New York: St. Martin's Press, 1988.

Sharp, Al. "'Biggest Thrill of Trip Was Watching Japan Loom From Ocean,' Says Georgian." *The Atlanta Constitution*, July 4, 1942

Sibley, Celestine. "Truelove Outshines Lamour, Sells $70,000 in Bonds Here." *The Atlanta Constitution*, July 4, 1942.

Statham, Frances Patton. *Mountain Legacy*. Atlanta: Cherokee Publishing Company, 1999.

Truelove, Denver V. Diary. March 31, 1942-June 25, 1942. Blanche Truelove Bowen private collection.

Vardeman, Johnny. "Hall County WWII hero helped US turn tide in the Pacific." *The Gainesville Times*. April 11, 2004.

Wooldridge, E.T. *Carrier Warfare in the Pacific*. Washington, DC: Smithsonian Institution Press, 1993.

Joyce, Todd. The Official Website of the Doolittle Tokyo Raiders. www.doolittleraider.com

"Atlanta's July 4 An Inspiration, Truelove Says." *Atlanta Constitution*, July 5, 1942.

"D. V. Truelove Is Promoted to Captaincy." *Atlanta Constitution*, December 23, 1942.

"Georgia Hero of Tokyo Raid 'Just a Country Boy,' Mother Says." Associated Press. *Atlanta Constitution*, May 20, 1942.

"Psychological Blow Seen in Raid on Japan." Associated Press. *Atlanta Constitution*, April 24, 1942.

Additional material was drawn from interviews with Blanche Truelove Bowen, Carroll V. Glines, David J. Thatcher, James Bower, Russell Jacobs, and Zheng Weiyong.

Photo Credits

All U.S. Air Force Archives photos are abbreviated as USAF.

All U.S. Navy Archives photos are abbreviated as USN.

All U.S. Army Signal Command photos are abbreviated as USASC.

All of the above USAF, USN, and USASC photos, along with President Roosevelt's photo in chapter one are works in the public domain in the United States because they are works of the United States Federal Government under the terms of Title 17, Chapter 1, Section 105 of the US Code.

The Tablets of the Missing photograph in chapter seven is courtesy of the American Battle Monuments Commission.

The B-25 photo is credited to Bo Burnette, author. The Truelove family photo is courtesy of Mrs. Blanche Truelove Bowen. All of the photographs in chapter eight are credited to Bo Burnette, author.

The Doolittle Tokyo Raiders' crest is used with the permission of the Doolittle Tokyo Raiders Association, Inc.

The Tabbystone Press logo is copyright © 2012 Tabbystone Press, all rights reserved.

Index

20-cent bombsight, *27, 37, 39*

310th Bomb Group, *58*

428th Squadron, *58*

Air Medal with Three Oak Leaf Cluster, *60*

Alameda Naval Base, California, *29*

Allied forces, *13, 15, 43, 44, 61*

Allied nations, *13*

American Campaign Medal, *60*

Army Air Corps, *18, 23, 57*

Axis powers, *13, 26, 58*

B-25, *16, 25, 26, 27, 29, 36, 40, 74, 97*

Barr, George, *61, 92*

Bower, William "Bill", *58, 62, 75*

Carthage, Tunisia, *61*

Chiang Kai-Shek, Generalissimo, *47*

Chiang, Madame May Ling Soong, *47, 48, 49, 50*

China, *13, 30, 33, 37, 40, 41, 45, 47, 49, 56, 79, 82, 92*

Chinese Air Force Medal, *60*

Chuchow, *30, 41, 43, 45, 46*

Chuhsien. *See* Chuchow

Chungking, *30, 47, 51*

Clermont, Georgia, *19, 20*

Cole, Richard, *38, 75*

Crews
  Crew #1, *77*
  Crew #10, *86*
  Crew #11, *87*
  Crew #12, *88*
  Crew #13, *89*
  Crew #14, *90*
  Crew #15, *91*
  Crew #16, *92*
  Crew #2, *78*
  Crew #3, *79*
  Crew #4, *80*
  Crew #5, *81*
  Crew #6, *82*
  Crew #7, *83*
  Crew #8, *84*
  Crew #9, *85*

Defense Medal, *60*

Denver, Colorado, *24*

DeShazer, Jacob D., *18, 61, 62, 92*

Distinguished Flying Cross, *52, 53, 60*

Doolittle Raiders
  Captured Raiders, *56, 61*
  Crest, *73, 74*

Reunions, *68, 69, 75*

Doolittle, James H. "Jimmy", *17, 38, 53, 68, 73, 94*

Eglin Field, Florida, *26, 28, 29*

Egypt, *51*

Emmens, Robert, *56*

England, *58*

Enterprise, U.S.S., *31, 32*

Foreign Service Medal, *60*

Georgia, United States, *21, 28, 67, 75*

Glines, Carroll V., *8, 62, 75, 93, 95*

Goblets, *62, 69, 71*

Greening, C. Ross, *27, 37, 87*

Griffin, Thomas, *75*

Gwinnett County Veterans Memorial Museum, Lawrenceville, Georgia, *67, 74*

Helena, Montana, *55*

Hengyang, *47*

Hirohito, Emperor, *43*

Hite, Robert L., *61, 92*

Hornet, U.S.S., *8, 11, 29, 30, 31, 32, 36, 37, 38, 41, 47, 67*

India, *51, 79, 86*

Japan, *13, 14, 15, 17, 30, 31, 32, 33, 38, 39, 40, 48, 49, 58, 60, 61, 73, 93*

Jones, David M., *35, 37, 38, 39, 40, 41, 42, 45, 81*

Kobe, *32, 37*

Lamour, Dorothy, *55*

Lawson, Ted W., *31, 32, 75*

Low, Francis S., *16*

Lula, Georgia, *18, 21, 51, 53, 65, 66, 74*

Manske, Joseph W., *35, 37, 38, 42, 45,* 81

McClellan Field, California, *28, 29*

McGurl, Eugene "Gene", *35, 40, 81*

Mediterranean Sea, *58*

Miami, Florida, *52, 68*

Mitscher, Marc A. "Pete", *36*

Nagoya, *37*

Navy, *14, 16, 27, 97*

Nielsen, Chase J., *61*

Nigeria, *51*

Nitto Maru, 32

Norden bombsight, *27*

North Africa, *58, 61, 78*

Osaka, *37*

Pearl Harbor, *13, 14, 15, 16*

Pendleton, Oregon, *24*

Purple Heart, *60*

Rabun Gap-Nacoochee Junior College, *21, 23, 24*

Randolph Field, Texas, *23*

Ritchie, Addie Corn, *22*

Ritchie, Dr. Andrew Jackson, *22*

Roosevelt, Franklin D., *14, 15, 16, 18, 21, 53*

Ruptured Duck, The, *46*

Saylor, Edward, *75*

Tablets of the Missing, *61*, *97*

Thatcher, David, *47*, *75*, *83*, *95*

Thirty Seconds Over Tokyo, *75*

Tokyo, *30*, *32*, *33*, *37*, *38*, *43*, *44*, *62*, *68*, *75*, *93*, *94*, *95*, *97*

Tokyo Bay, *39*

Truelove, Blanche, *7*, *19*, *20*, *21*, *28*, *59*, *62*, *65*, *95*

Truelove, Clyde, *19*

Truelove, Denver, *7*, *9*, *18*, *19*, *20*, *21*, *22*, *23*, *24*, *25*, *28*, *30*, *31*, *32*, *35*, *36*, *37*, *38*, *39*, *40*, *42*, *43*, *45*, *46*, *47*, *48*, *50*, *51*, *52*, *53*, *54*, *55*, *56*, *57*, *58*, *59*, *60*, *61*, *62*, *65*, *67*, *68*, *71*, *73*, *74*, *75*, *76*, *81*, *95*

Truelove, Gertrude, *19*, *53*

Tucson, Arizona, *69*

Tuscaloosa, Alabama, *23*

United States, *5*, *13*, *14*, *15*, *17*, *24*, *28*, *30*, *61*

University of Georgia, *23*

Veterans Memorial Park, Lula, Georgia, *65*, *74*

War bonds, *54*, *57*, *60*

White, T. Robert "Doc", *47*

Wilder, Rodney R. "Hoss", *35*, *40*

World War I, *13*

World War II, *9*, *13*, *44*, *60*, *93*, *94*

Yokohama, *37*

York, Edward "Ski", *56*

About the Author

Bo Burnette, the great-great nephew of Denver Truelove, was, like Denver, born and raised in Georgia. He lives and breathes stories and has several books with his name on their covers, most notably World War II biography *Denver and the Doolittle Raid*, middle-grade mystery *The Lighthouse Thief*, and *The Reinhold Chronicles* trilogy.

The opening chapter of *The Reinhold Chronicles* trilogy

Arliss, the sixteen-year-old princess of Reinhold, despises the class boundaries which plague her city on a hill. When her father the king forbids her friendship with the young peasant swordsman Philip, Arliss sets off on a quest to the heart of the land Reinhold, only to discover an evil more threatening and ancient than she could imagine.

The middle chapter of *The Reinhold Chronicles* trilogy

The clan of Reinhold fled from the Isle of Light thirteen years ago. Now—armed with her bow and determined to reclaim lost treasures—Princess Arliss wants to go back.

"I could hear the music again, and somehow it seemed louder than before."

Every day, Miss Erikson hears mysterious music coming from behind a locked door at the Lang School of Fine Arts. When the strict Mrs. Borg demands she leave the door alone, Miss Erikson's curiosity propels her to uncover the secrets of the ever-closed door. As she pursues the source of the inexplicable music, she must finally face the grief of the past she has long tried to ignore. (A 3,000-word short story by Bo Burnette)

A historic lighthouse. A suspect thief. An intolerable cousin.

The Fourth of July is always a big holiday on Saint Simons Island. But this year, while coping with a visit from his contrary cousin, 14-year-old Ethan discovers strange happenings at the historic lighthouse. Soon he is caught up in an unexpected adventure and a quest to save his beloved lighthouse.

www.ingramcontent.com/pod-product-compliance
Lightning Source LLC
Chambersburg PA
CBHW051849090426
42811CB00034B/2270/J